Austria

FRANKLIN WATTS
NEW YORK | LONDON | 1976
A FIRST BOOK

by Carol Zeman Rothkopf

Austria

Frontispiece: The beautiful mountains of Tyrol

Cover design by One + One Studio

All photographs are courtesy of the Austrian
National Tourist Office

Library of Congress Cataloging in Publication Data

Rothkopf, Carol Zeman.
    Austria.

    (A First book)
    Includes index.
    SUMMARY: Introduces the culture and his-
tory of Austria.
    1. Austria — Juvenile literature. [1. Austria]
I. Title.
DB17.R67   943.6   75–38675
ISBN 0–531–00842–8

For EZR
Tu, felix Austria, nube

1903195

Contents

OFFICIAL NAME:
Republik Österreich — Republic of Austria

AREA:
32,375 sq. mi. (83,850 sq. km.)

LOCATION:
Central Europe. Latitude — 46°30′ N to 49° N.
Longitude — 9°30′ E to 17° E.

CAPITAL:
Vienna

CHIEF CITIES:
Vienna, Graz, Salzburg, Innsbruck

POPULATION:
7,456,000 (est.)

LANGUAGE:
German

RELIGION:
Roman Catholic

NATIONAL HOLIDAY:
October 26, National Day

Essential Facts

NATIONAL ANTHEM:

Land der Berge, Land am Strom ("Land of Mountains, Land on the River")

GOVERNMENT:

Federal republic. Head of state — president. Head of government — chancellor. Legislature — bicameral (two houses): *Bundesrat* (upper house), *Nationalrat* (lower house).

POLITICAL PARTIES:

Socialist party
People's party
Freedom party

ECONOMY:

Chief mineral resources — coal, iron, magnesite, graphite, lead, zinc, copper, oil, bauxite. Chief agricultural products — wheat, rye, oats, barley, potatoes, sugar beets. Industries and products — iron and steel, aluminum, paper, chemicals, textiles, machinery and tools, electrical current. Chief imports — machinery and transportation equipment, coal and coke; wool and cotton. Chief exports — iron and steel, timber and wood, machinery and tools, paper, aluminum, electric current. Monetary unit: schilling (= about U.S. $0.06, 1975), made up of 100 groschen

You have lots of company if just hearing the word *Austria* makes you hum a waltz, see a vision of castles, dream of glorious pageants, hunger for heaps of whipped cream, or want to ski down more solid slopes of snow.

Austria is one of those countries whose people, history, and arts have added so much to the civilized world that it is hard to remember that it is really not a fairy-tale country at all but a small nation that jealously guards its neutrality on the frontier separating Western and Eastern Europe.

Austria's boundaries have changed often over the centuries, but nothing short of erasing the country from the map can change its strategic location in central Europe. Austria is at the crossroads of the major land routes. This simple fact has been of great importance from the dawn of Austria's history to this day.

For the Romans, the Danube River in Austria was a frontier defense line against barbarian invasions of their empire. The eighth-century French monarch Charlemagne made the territory his Ostmark — "east march" (frontier). To the early Holy Roman emperors of the German nation the region was Ostarichi — "east kingdom." The modern name of this ancient land is Republik Österreich — Republic of Austria — which, if translated accurately, means the "Republic of the East Kingdom." It is an appropriate

An Introduction

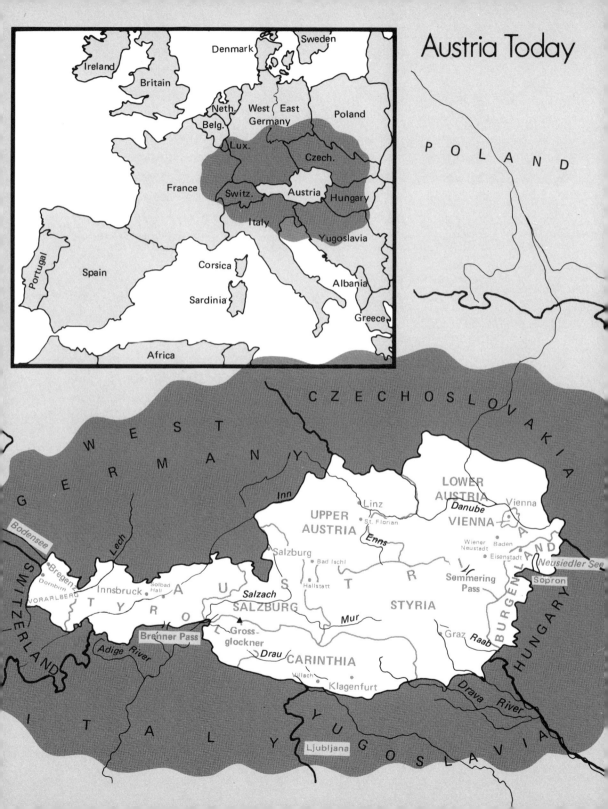

Austria Today

Inset map (Europe):

Ireland · Britain · Denmark · Sweden · Neth. · Belg. · Lux. · West Germany · East Germany · Poland · France · Switz. · Czech. · Austria · Hungary · Italy · Yugoslavia · Portugal · Spain · Corsica · Sardinia · Albania · Greece · Africa

Main map (Austria):

POLAND

CZECHOSLOVAKIA

WEST GERMANY

Bodensee · Inn · Lech · Linz · Danube · LOWER AUSTRIA · Vienna · UPPER AUSTRIA · St. Florian · Enns · VIENNA · Salzburg · Wiener Neustadt · Baden · Eisenstadt · Neusiedler See · Bregenz · Dornbirn · Bad Ischl · Semmering Pass · Sopron · VORARLBERG · Innsbruck · Solbad Hall · Hallstatt · BURGENLAND · Salzach · TYROL · SALZBURG · STYRIA · HUNGARY · Brenner Pass · Mur · Gross-glockner · Graz · Raab · Adige River · Drau · CARINTHIA · Villach · Klagenfurt · Drava River · SWITZERLAND · ITALY · Ljubljana · YUGOSLAVIA name for a nation that is a curious blend of modern democracy and ancient imperial splendor.

To people who remember the great expanse that was the Austrian empire until the end of World War I, the most remarkable fact about Austria is that it is now so small. The once-enormous territory that stretched from Poland in the north deep into Yugoslavia in the south, and embraced the lands between Germany and Russia, is now divided into many nations. In the center of these nations lies Austria, which is now not much larger than when Rudolf of Habsburg started to build the empire in the thirteenth century. Covering 32,375 square miles, Austria is about the size of Maine. As befits a neutral country, an equal number of Communist and non-Communist countries surround it.

Until 1919, when Austria's present boundaries were fixed, the empire was home to over 55 million people, who spoke more than fifteen different languages. Today the population numbers about 7.4 million, nearly all of whom are German-speaking. Most are members of the Roman Catholic Church.

The small size of both the population and the country suggests that Austria is simple and uncomplicated — an easy place to get to know. Because the Austrians are a hospitable and friendly people and because the land is mainly a straightforward mixture of soaring Alps and rolling hills, this is partly true. The complications of Austria stem from its long and important history and from the facts of present-day life in the small republic. Modern Austria is a federation of nine states — Vorarlberg, Tyrol, Styria, Salzburg, Upper Austria, Lower Austria, Carinthia, Burgenland, and Vienna. Each of the nine states, or provinces, as they are often called in English, has its own distinctive setting, history, and customs. Visiting each of the nine states is like traveling to nine different mini-countries.

VORARLBERG
THE WESTERNMOST PROVINCE

With its territory of about one thousand square miles (roughly the same as Rhode Island) Vorarlberg is the smallest of Austria's nine provinces except for the capital city of Vienna, which has special status. Vorarlberg, whose name means "in front of Arlberg" — Arlberg is a range of the Alps — is also the westernmost of the Austrian states. Vorarlberg was added to Austria in bits and pieces between the fourteenth and the sixteenth century.

The tiny province, with its lakes and mountains, is a good place to start a tour of Austria. It offers all that is thought of as typically Austrian — beautiful scenery, colorful traditions, delicious food, all kinds of cultural and sporting events, and a good cross section of the country's agricultural and industrial life.

The Vorarlbergers like to say that Noah's Ark finally reached dry land in their soaring mountains. It is more certain that the region has been settled since the Stone Age. The ancestors of the present residents were German tribesmen who came to the region in about the third century B.C.

In Vorarlberg, as everywhere in Austria, the Romans contributed to the history of the land. For example, the capital of

The Nine Provinces

The waterfront theater at Bregenz

Vorarlberg, Bregenz, which is perched above the Bodensee (or Lake Constance as it is usually called in English), began its history as a Roman trading center. The lower part of the city, stretching along the lakefront, is the center of the newer part of the city. It is here that audiences gather in an amphitheater each summer for the Bregenz Music Festival. The festival is exciting for its music, of course, but also because part of the stage actually floats on the waters of the lake.

Tucked away in the mountains of Vorarlberg are charming old villages with strange and beautiful names like Au and Egg, Dornbirn and Feldkirch. Here, in the mountain villages and the valley towns, you will still see people proudly wearing their traditional costumes — at least to attend church on Sunday. Experts can tell the difference between the costumes of each town, but for the visitor the costumes also serve as a reminder that Vorarlberg is an important center of textile manufacturing, one of Austria's most important industries. Another vital industry is based on the water rushing down the steep slopes of the Alps. The water is harnessed as hydroelectric power, or "white coal," as it is more poetically known. White coal is a major source of energy in modern Austria.

Snow gleaming on the mountains and carpets of beautiful alpine flowers near sweet-smelling pine forests are among the biggest attractions for visitors who come to ski, to climb the mountains, or just to enjoy being two to three thousand feet above sea level. Tucked away in the mountains there are surprising sights — such as the old palace and fortress at Hohenems, Götzis with its crumbling castle, and the Schattenburg castle, which is Feldkirch's special attraction. There is much more to see in Vorarlberg, but for the traveler discovering Austria the road to take is from Warth through the magnificent Lech valley into the province of Tyrol.

TYROL:
THE PICTURE-POSTCARD
PROVINCE

Tyrol, like Vorarlberg, is a land with extraordinary mountain scenery. The fact that for centuries it has welcomed travelers may explain why, when you say "Austria," the picture-postcard view that pops into mind is a view of Tyrol.

Tyrol — or Tirol, as it is known in German — has a population of slightly more than 500,000 living in an area of nearly 5,000 square miles. The province was settled in waves by Illyrians, Celts, Romans, and finally Germanic tribes, including the Lombards and Franks. Tyrol's history since those remote times has been extremely complicated — partly because of its important location near the vital Brenner Pass through the Alps into Italy, partly because of its geographic importance to the rulers of Austria, and partly because of its once-valuable silver mines.

From the eleventh century to 1801 South Tyrol was ruled by the bishops of Trent and Brixen. The northern Tyrol — roughly the region of the present province — became a part of Austria in 1363 when the Countess Margarete Maultasch gave Rudolf IV of Austria ". . . the land on the Etsch and the Inn valley with Schloss Tirol and all else appertaining thereto." No one is quite sure what the Countess Maultasch looked like, but her last name means "bag mouth" and there are those who say that the pictures of the Ugly Duchess in *Alice in Wonderland* could have been based on this lady's unusual face.

In the early nineteenth century, during the Napoleonic wars, Tyrol was given to the king of Bavaria — an act that was violently resisted by patriotic peasants under the leadership of Andreas Hofer. Hofer became a national hero for his efforts, even though they were not successful and it was only after Napoleon's defeat in 1814 that Austria regained control of the province. This arrangement lasted only until 1919, when South Tyrol was given to Italy as part of the war settlement. Even now, many years after South Tyrol passed to Italy, there is still strong feeling in the area about who is the rightful owner of the region.

Although Tyrol is clearly rich in history, patriotic feeling, and mountains, it is poor in farmland. The most important industries are forestry, salt mining in the region of Solbad Hall, and some manufacturing around Innsbruck, Landeck, and Kufstein.

Coming to Innsbruck, Tyrol's most visited and historic city, one is surprised to see so much evidence of the twentieth century in a setting of such Alpine beauty. There are high-rise apartments, factories, and superhighways, as well as the sites of two winter Olympic Games (the ninth, in 1964, and the twelfth, in 1976).

One of the most famous sights in Innsbruck is the Goldenes Dachl ("Golden Roof"), really a gilded copper roof that glitters like gold on a house that was built for one of the dukes of Tyrol. The Goldenes Dachl is in the heart of Innsbruck's old town, where one begins to see and sense the city's past. Innsbruck means "Inn Bridge" in German, which suggests correctly that the city began as a trading post on the Inn River. By the time the countess gave Tyrol to the Austrian king in the fourteenth century, the city was one of the most important in the realm.

Innsbruck was a favorite residence of two of Austria's rulers — Maximilian I (emperor 1493–1519) and Maria Theresa (ruled 1740–1780). Maximilian liked Innsbruck so well that he planned to be buried there and to build himself a tomb and church to rival anything ever built in Europe. This Court Church (Hofkirche) was finished in 1563, and for some reason Maximilian's body was

The emperor Maximilian I's tomb is guarded by his family and "ancestors," including King Arthur of England (*left*).

never moved there from the church in Wiener Neustadt, south of Vienna, where he had been buried. Maximilian's elaborate tomb still stands, however, surrounded by the large bronze statues of twenty-eight of his family and ancestors (some real, some imaginary like King Arthur).

But there is much more to Innsbruck and all Tyrol than memories. This area is easily one of the most beautiful in all of Europe — a winter sports center and a popular goal for summer vacationers. It is the ideal place to learn to toboggan, ice-skate, or ski. If you get really good at skiing, you can try your skill on the glacier at Obergurgl or the summer skiing in Hochgurgl.

Tyrol is also the natural place to put on the traditional Austrian walking costume — lederhosen for men, dirndls for women — and just walk slowly up the handiest mountain. Once atop a hill or mountain, open your mouth wide and yodel, a form of singing the Tyroleans have helped make famous amid their echoing mountains.

SALZBURG:
LAND OF MINES, MOUNTAINS,
AND MUSIC

Moving eastward across Austria, one reaches Salzburg. This 2,762-square-mile province is almost completely and beautifully mountainous. Here the Hohe Tauern and Salzburg Alps soar above the land and provide gorgeous scenery, the rushing waters that produce power for industry, and a wealth of mineral resources ranging from gold to salt.

The most important word in the vocabulary of the province is *Salz*, "salt." The province *and* its capital city are both called

Salzburg, which means "Salt City." The city is located on the *Salzach* River, and part of the region known as the *Salzkammergut* — Estate of the Salt Chamber — lies within the province.

Nowadays we take salt totally for granted and would be very surprised if we did not have a shaker full of it on the table at mealtimes. This was not always the case. In ancient times salt was rare. Because it was valuable as a seasoning and a food preservative, it was often used as money. Naturally governments carefully supervised the mining and distribution of salt in olden days. In fact, until the mid-nineteenth century the Salzkammergut (which also includes part of Upper Austria and Styria) was closed to visitors because of its valuable salt mines.

Salzburg is also known for its typically Austrian collection of castles and fortresses and churches, and for its music. This is the land of Mozart and of music festivals, of the Trapp family of singers, and of the play and movie *The Sound of Music*. Curiously, the state that now honors all its musicians was not too kind to them when they were residents. Wolfgang Amadeus Mozart, who was born in Salzburg in 1756 and even spent some years as concertmaster to the archbishop of Salzburg, was received with the most warmth and honor in Prague (now the capital of Czechoslovakia). The Trapp family, as theater- and moviegoers know, fled from Hitler's troops to find a welcome in the United States.

If Salzburg was not too generous to its most famous son, Mozart, during his lifetime, it has more than made up for it — if not to him, at least to his admirers. In the province's capital city there are both a bridge and a square named for the great composer. Since 1842 a music festival has been held, mainly in his honor, each summer, and each January there is a Mozart Festival. In between times there are concerts featuring his music — even the local belltower plays Mozartean tunes.

Visitors must put on special overalls to
travel through the eerie world of the salt mines.

A Mozartean performance at the
Salzburg Marionette Theater

There is more to the history of Salzburg, of course, than salt and Mozart. The first settlers were probably Celts, but it was the Romans who gave the name of Juvavum to the trading post we know as the city of Salzburg. The Romans were driven out by Goths and Huns, and little is known of the city's life during that period. By the early ninth century Salzburg was the seat of a Catholic archbishop. For more than one thousand years the archbishops of Salzburg were the most powerful German-speaking leaders of the Church — as well as imperial Austrian princes. It was not until the early nineteenth century that Salzburg's government passed from the leaders of the Church to laymen.

Outside the city of Salzburg, at Hallein (of saltmine fame), one can visit the burial place of Franz Gruber, the composer of the Christmas carol "Silent Night, Holy Night," or seek out a peaceful mountain scene and simply listen to the birds. Students of caves come to the province to explore the Tantalhöhle caves in the Hagengebirge mountains, which were not discovered until 1948, or to tour the thrilling Eisriesenwelt — the "Ice Giants' World"— a fantastic series of ice caves that contain one frozen marvel after another over a distance of about thirty miles.

There are two other natural wonders that no visitor to Salzburg can afford to miss. One is the spectacular 1,250-foot Krimml waterfall, which is the highest in Europe. The other is Austria's highest mountain, the 12,460-foot Grossglockner ("Big Bell"), which Salzburg shares with the neighboring provinces of Tyrol and Carinthia. Not too long ago, the only way to get to the top was on foot, but now engineers have designed and built a road that loops up the slopes until at last you are at the top — and all Austria (almost) is at your feet.

CARINTHIA:
THE SOUTHERNMOST
PROVINCE

The 3,681-square-mile province of Carinthia, or Kärnten, as it is known in German, is typically Austrian in its scenic mixture of mountains and lakes. Unlike the other Austrian provinces, however, it has a large non-German-speaking minority, made up of Slovenes whose ancestors settled in the region centuries ago. The presence of the Slovenes shows one is near Austria's border with the Yugoslav republic of Slovenia. At the end of World War I, Austria had to give slices of Carinthia to the newly formed nation of Yugoslavia and to Italy. Statesmen may be able to change boundaries easily, but centuries of tradition do not disappear quite so fast. In fact, Slovenia's captial, Ljubljana, still looks almost as Austrian as Carinthia's capital city, Klagenfurt.

Despite the details of geography, history, and customs that are shared by Carinthia and Slovenia, the Austrian province has a long, proud history as a separate political state. The richly forested region, with its wealth of mineral resources (lead, zinc, iron, and coal) and its farmlands of the Drau River region has been settled since prehistoric times. Indeed, what may be the largest Celtic settlement in Europe is still being excavated at Magdalensberg in Carinthia. Here, as elsewhere in Austria, the Celts were followed by the Romans, who are credited with discovering some of the province's spas — mineral springs — to which people still come for the rest and the supposedly health-giving waters.

The next wave of settlement was Slovenian, and by 976 the independent duchy of Carantania had been established. Independence did not last long. In the thirteenth century, Carantania was absorbed by the then powerful kingdom of Bohemia (now part of Czechoslovakia). In the early fourteenth century it became a crownland of Austria.

From the excavations at Magdalensberg to the museums and palaces of Klagenfurt, one can trace all of Carinthia's history. There are Roman ruins in the Glan River valley, which is also the place to see the Herzogstuhl ("Duke's Chair") — one of the two stone thrones on which the Carantanian dukes were crowned. (The other throne, the Fürstenstein — "Prince's Chair" — is in a museum in Klagenfurt.) Other fascinating landmarks of the Middle Ages include Friesach, where plays are staged; Gurk, with its renowned old cathedral; the castle of Hochosterwitz; and, last but far from least, the capital city of Klagenfurt.

Klagenfurt's oldest buildings date to the thirteenth century, but its best-known feature comes straight out of a fairy tale. It is the *Lindwurm* — dragon — a bronze statue in the main square. To students of literature, Klagenfurt is better known as the birthplace of Austria's greatest modern novelist, Robert Musil, whose four-volume book *The Man Without Qualities* is a complex and gripping portrait of the last year that imperial Austria was at peace.

Carinthia's second-largest city, Villach, grew up around one of the mineral springs discovered by the Romans. Today it is known for its churches, Renaissance buildings, and museums, and as a leading industrial and rail center.

Many people think of Carinthia as a place to visit in summer because its forested slopes and deep, blue lakes — the Wörther See, Ossiacher See, Millstätter See, Weissen See, Faaker See, and Klopeiner See — are at their most beautiful. But Carinthia's beauty and its interesting festivals fill the calendar all year long.

The Erzberg — Iron Mountain — attracts
tourists as well as miners to its terraced slopes.

One of the most unusual festivals is held in late May or early June, in Weitensfeld. It is a kind of joust called the *Kranzelreiten*. The men of the village, on horseback, try to spear a ring. This recalls the time in the Middle Ages when an epidemic of the plague left only one marriageable girl in the village and the three surviving males had to compete for her hand — or so the legend goes. The reward for today's competitors is a wreath, or *Kranzel,* as it is known in German.

Carinthia's calendar also includes ski races on the Grossglockner glaciers in June, summer music and theater festivals all over the province, and historic pageants on the lakes and in many villages — a blend composed of equal parts of history, scenery, and fun.

STYRIA:
THE SECOND-LARGEST
PROVINCE

Sloping down from the high Alps to the hills of Burgenland is the province of Styria. Styria, like Carinthia, shares a border with Yugoslavia, to which it, too, ceded land in 1919. All of Styria's other borders are firmly Austrian.

Styria — Steiermark, in German — covers 6,326 square miles, which gives it the distinction of being the second-largest Austrian province. Its capital city, Graz, also ranks second in size after Vienna. In most other ways Styria is unique and does not play second fiddle to any part of the republic.

Styria ranks as Austria's prime source of mineral wealth because it is in this province that Austria's largest deposits of iron, coal, and magnesite are found. The Erzberg — "Iron Mountain" —

One of the most popular sights in
Graz is the great armor collection.

is a nearly 5,000-foot-high open-faced iron mine at whose terraced slopes men have been picking and blasting for centuries. Nowadays the raw iron ore is converted to steel in the blast furnaces and rolling mills of Donawitz. Styria is an important agricultural center, as well. Cattle graze on the mountain slopes and in the valleys. The mountains are also a valuable source of timber.

Along with its mineral wealth, Styria offers the traveler not only that Austrian staple — mountains and still more mountains — but also the beauty of such river valleys as those cut by the Mur, Enns, and Raab rivers, plus a full share of history, castles, legends, and monuments.

Graz, the provincial capital, which is on the Mur River, was probably founded by the Romans. It was a good choice for a frontier settlement because it is located on one of the easiest routes into Austria. As a result, Graz has been the goal of many invaders — the Hungarians under the leadership of Matthias Corvinus in 1481, the Turks in 1529 and 1532, and, most seriously, the French under Napoleon in 1797 and 1805. The French were the first successful conquerors of the city.

The only part of the city's old fortifications on the Schlossberg ("Castle Hill") that survived the French siege and occupation was the clock tower, which is now the symbol of Graz, as the dragon is of Klagenfurt. Down below the Schlossberg, the city's most famous landmark is the Landhaus, the Renaissance state parliament building. In part of this building is the Styrian Armory, which is considered one of the finest collections of its kind in the world.

The beauties of Graz may have provided the inspiration for Styria's most famous citizen — the architect Johann Bernhard

This glittering baroque altar at Mariazell in Styria was designed by Fischer von Erlach.

Fischer von Erlach (1656–1723). Fischer von Erlach is considered one of the greatest baroque architects. He designed the tomb of the Habsburg emperor Ferdinand II in Graz Cathedral, the Royal Library and the Karlskirche in Vienna, and the Church of the Trinity in Salzburg.

It is more difficult to describe baroque architecture than to look at it. Baroque buildings are a remarkable blend of ornamentation — swirling columns and exquisite decorations — with setting. A real baroque masterpiece always seems to have grown out of the land on which it is built. The setting leaves you plenty of space to admire every curve and every angle. But as one Austrian has said, it may just be easier to think of baroque architecture as a marvelous heap of whipped cream neatly decorated with the near-gold of eggyolks.

This typically Austrian emphasis on food, delicious food, leads one naturally out of Graz to the gentle hills of the Windische Bühel, where some of the best Austrian wine grapes are grown. West of the Windische Bühel is the small town of Piber, a mecca for horsemen. The Lippizaner horses are raised and receive their first training in Piber before they are sent north to the Spanish Riding Academy in Vienna, where experts teach these handsome animals literally to dance.

North of Piber are the mountains that separate Styria from Vienna. They are a vacation land for the Viennese and are known for fine skiing, the Semmering Pass (one of Europe's first railroad tunnels through the mountains), and water that Viennese drink and proclaim to be the best in the world. But it is in the east — in the long slice of land called Burgenland — that Vienna's important market basket is located in Austria's most untypical province.

BURGENLAND: AUSTRIA'S YOUNGEST PROVINCE

Burgenland, one of the smallest Austrian provinces, covers only 1,531 square miles and is the youngest of the nine. It is the one place in the country that does not look a bit as one expects Austria to look. Here one needs neither skis nor hiking boots, because Burgenland is a region of rolling, fertile farmland where three thousand feet above sea level is considered a dizzy height. Instead of cattle grazing on the mountain slopes, there are productive fruit and vegetable farms.

Burgenland's political association with Vienna and all of Austria is new, compared to the nation's very long history. In 1922 a slice of Hungary was transferred to Austria. The exception to this transfer was Burgenland's capital city, Sopron (formerly Ödenburg), and the area around it, whose citizens voted to remain Hungarians. The result is a curious dent in Burgenland's eastern frontier where the capital used to be.

The small town of Eisenstadt is now Burgenland's capital. But what Eisenstadt lacks in size it more than makes up in musical history. Here Franz Joseph Haydn (1732–1809), one of Austria's greatest composers, lived while he was musical director for the Hungarian Esterházy princes. Both he and Franz Liszt, the great nineteenth-century composer, are commemorated in a museum built in Haydn's home in Eisenstadt.

Not far from Eisenstadt is the Neusiedlersee, the largest shallow lake in central Europe. Although the lake covers about 130 square miles, its average depth is only five feet. Sometimes, if the wind is blowing hard, parts of the lake dry up. Nearly all the lake is surrounded by a belt of reeds, which may make it a bit difficult

Ice-boating is the winter sport
on the Neusiedlersee.

to go swimming but which provide a wonderful hiding place for birds. In fact, the Neusiedlersee is one of the most remarkable bird refuges in Europe. A familiar sight in towns all around the lake is the stork, which really does nest on top of chimneys. And geese still wander down the streets near the farms as if they were the first citizens of the land.

The picturesque Burgenland countryside with its wealth of wildlife, its fertile farms, and its vineyards is now as peaceful as it looks, but this was not always the case. Burgenland, like all of Austria, has seen more than its share of violent history. For about one thousand years this area stood squarely in the path of advancing armies. Castles such as Forchtenstein, Schlaining, and Lockenhaus are silent witnesses to the past.

Moving westward from Burgenland across the trails blazed by invaders long ago, one comes to the historic heart of the nation — the provinces of Upper and Lower Austria and the great capital city, Vienna.

UPPER AUSTRIA:
LAND OF HILLS
AND FORESTS

Oberösterreich, as the province is called in German, is (along with *Niederösterreich,* Lower Austria) the historic center of Austria. It is in this 4,625-square-mile province that the soaring Alps begin their slow descent to the rolling hills of Vienna and the plains of Hungary. The province's name comes from the fact that it is above the Enns River — that is, upstream of where the Enns joins the Danube — while Lower Austria is below the river.

Upper Austria's most gorgeous scenery is in its share of the Salzkammergut (Estate of the Salt Chamber), where lakes, forests, meadows, and mountains offer a hiding place from the twentieth century. The region's quiet beauty is obviously a gift of nature, but it was the government's reluctance to let visitors into the salt-rich area that kept it hidden for so long. It was the nineteenth-century Emperor Francis Joseph (Franz Josef, in German) who opened the area to visitors and gave the Salzkammergut extra popularity by making his summer home at the now-famous resort Bad Ischl. Music historians are more familiar with this spa town as the site of one of the homes of Franz Lehár, whose operettas, such as *The Merry Widow* (1905), are one of the reasons foreigners think of Austria as a nation of singing, fun-loving aristocrats living in a wonderful never-never land.

The oldest settlement in Upper Austria, Hallstatt, was built on the lake of that name. Houses perched on stilts sunk into the water provided Stone Age men and their families with the nation's first fortresses against invaders. These early settlers were probably attracted to the area by the abundance of salt. These and other details of the lives of these early Upper Austrians have been carefully reconstructed from bones and relics found in the region and are displayed in a fascinating museum in Hallstatt.

Probably the most famous piece of music ever written in Austria is Johann Strauss II's *Blue Danube Waltz*. The beautiful melody should go through one's head in Upper Austria because it is here, at Passau, that the river enters Austria from Germany. And it is on the Danube that the province's capital city, Linz, was founded by the Romans as the settlement of Lentia. Today Linz ranks as Austria's third-largest city, after Vienna and Graz. It is an important

The Danube River — the main waterway
across Austria to the east

industrial center, with iron and steel works, chemical plants, and a bustling port on the river.

Just south of Linz is St. Florian, a small town that seems to contain all that is thought of as most Austrian, since it combines a legend, great age, baroque architecture, and, of course, a resounding musical note. The legend concerns Florian, a man of the fourth century, who chose to drown himself rather than worship the pagan gods of the Romans. The Church honored his defiance by naming him a saint. On the site of what was believed to be St. Florian's tomb, Augustinian monks built a monastery that is widely known both for its baroque architecture and as the burial place of the nineteenth-century composer Anton Bruckner.

It was in St. Florian that the Pümmerin — the great bell of St. Stephen's Cathedral in Vienna — was recast after it was damaged in World War II. Properly called *Regina Austriae*, "the queen of Austria," the bell was rehung in St. Stephen's tower with great ceremony, while inside the cathedral the first music to be played was Bruckner's *Te Deum*.

LOWER AUSTRIA:
THE LARGEST
PROVINCE

Whether one enters Lower Austria by way of the Danube River or by airplane, landing at Vienna's Schwechat Airport, one has arrived at the center of Austrian history and culture. Even the most patriotic Tyrolean or Styrian would tell you that you have not been in Austria if you have not been in *Niederösterreich*.

The province's area of 7,402 square miles makes it the largest of the Austrian provinces. Lower Austria's location, size, and prosperity make it the pivot around which the country turns. The national capital, Vienna, is actually inside the borders of Lower Austria and also serves as the province's capital.

Lower Austria is the country's leading producer of farm goods and a vital industrial center. If the Burgenland is known as Vienna's market basket, then Lower Austria is rightfully called the nation's granary. As well as fields of wheat, there are vegetable gardens and miles of vineyards — some of which probably date back to those tireless explorers, conquerors, and vine-planters, the Romans. Among the vineyards in the region of Zistersdorf, oil derricks have sprung up, providing Austria with at least part of the oil and natural gas it needs to run modern machines.

The most important industrial center in Lower Austria is Wiener Neustadt, south of Vienna. Historically this city is remembered as the place where Emperor Maximilian is buried instead of in his elaborate tomb in Innsbruck. It is also the site of the imperial military school that was founded in the eighteenth century by Maria Theresa. Today, despite heavy bombing during World War II, Wiener Neustadt is again best known for such products as locomotives and heavy machinery.

In Lower Austria, as elsewhere in Austria, there is enough to keep visitors occupied for a lifetime of vacations. There is not only the lovely scenery that one expects to find but also what may be the densest collection of castles, fortresses, and abbeys to be found anywhere in Europe. It is estimated that of the thousand or more such structures that once stood in Lower Austria, over five hundred remain. The question is not what to see but what one can afford not to see!

Entering Lower Austria by way of the Danube from Linz, one would pass Seitenstetten, an abbey founded by Benedictine monks in the early twelfth century, and Persenbeug, where there has been a castle since the ninth century but which is best known as the birthplace of the last ruling Habsburg, Charles I (Karl I, in German). Farther down the river is Melk, one of the most famous abbeys in Austria. It was founded as a fort in the tenth century, the Benedictine order rebuilt it as an abbey in the twelfth century, and in the eighteenth century it was rebuilt once more — in the baroque style, of course. The vast library at Melk is a national treasure containing manuscripts that go back as far in time as the original fort.

Continuing downriver, one comes to the ruins of Dürnstein, where, as the undying legend has it, Richard the Lion-Hearted of England was held captive from January, 1192, to March, 1193, by the wicked duke of Austria, until he was found by his faithful minstrel Blondel and set free for a huge ransom. Beyond the ruins of Dürnstein at the edge of the Vienna Woods is the abbey called Klosterneuburg, which is known for its great art treasures.

In the other river valleys and atop the rolling hills of the region there are many more such fine old buildings. All of them were built as both homes and fortresses or monasteries and fortresses, since Lower Austria was on the direct line of invasion from the north and east during the centuries when land wars were sadly regular events in Europe.

To escape from such unhappy memories, one has only to start humming again — this time a few notes from Johann Strauss II's second-most-famous waltz, *Tales from the Vienna Woods*, and one is transported to the forested hills outside Vienna into what is surely one of the most beautiful natural parks open to the citizens of any city in the world. Moving south from the Vienna Woods, one comes to the string of small grape-growing and wine-producing communities — Sievering, Nussdorf, Grinzing — where the Viennese come during spring and summer to taste the *Heurige* — the new wine.

South of Vienna the vineyards continue along the well-named *Weinstrasse*, "Wine Street," and lead one to still another spa founded by the Romans, which is known simply as Baden ("Bath"). The waters of Baden's sulfurous hot springs have been taken as a cure by such noblemen as Russia's Czar Peter the Great and inspired commoners from Mozart to Beethoven to Johann Strauss II — as well as more ordinary mortals.

In the region east of Vienna, called the Marchfeld, one is at the ancient frontier of the Ostmark. It is here that the Romans built their fortress and regional capital at Carnuntum. And it was here in 1278 that Rudolf I of Habsburg killed his chief rival, Ottokar II of Bohemia. This event helped to decide the course of European history for 640 years. Of course, it is in Vienna itself that the great power and glory that were the Habsburgs' are still most evident. From that city they long ruled as "King of Bohemia and Hungary, Archduke of Austria, Duke of Styria, Count of Tyrol, and Lord of Trieste . . ."; and so on for paragraphs of imperial pomp and splendor.

VIENNA: IMPERIAL CAPITAL OF THE REPUBLIC

A map maker will tell you that Vienna covers about 160 square miles in the broad valley carved by the Danube between the Alps and the Carpathian mountains. A diplomat will note that Vienna is the capital of both Austria and Lower Austria but has the status of a separate state within the republic. A professor of history will observe that Vienna sums up Austrian history from the Stone Age to the present. But for a cabdriver, his city is, in the words of a popular song, "where the angels go on vacation."

Vienna is, of course, a blend of all these views. A remarkably beautiful and historic city, it is home to about one fifth of the entire population of Austria. And Vienna has its share of industry, as well as being the center of government. Among its more important products are machines, textiles, chemicals, and furniture. Large oil refineries, distilleries, and breweries also play a vital role in the city's economy, as does the manufacture of such things as clothing, leather goods, costume jewelry, and ceramics. Not surprisingly, considering its beauty and its wealth of historic landmarks, Vienna also derives a large portion of its income from tourism. **1903195**

Even when life on the eastern frontier of Europe was far less peaceful than it is now, Vienna was a magnet for settlement. Relics like the curious little figure called the "Venus of Willendorf" suggest that there were settlers as early as 20,000 B.C. By the time the Romans came north in the first century B.C., the Celts were well established and had named their small center in the Danube valley Vindobona, which may mean "white fields." It was the Romans, of course, who built the first good roads and fortifications and who introduced the law and, by the end of their rule, the Christian faith.

Between the fall of the Roman Empire and the eleventh century A.D., the city suffered its share of barbarian invasions and destruction. But in the twelfth century Austria's first ruling family, the Babenbergs, came to power and set the city on its course to fame and grandeur. It was the Babenbergs who began the building of St. Stephen's just outside the wall of the oldest part of the city, the *Innere Stadt* ("Inner City") and it was they who built the first royal palace, Am Hof, within the walls.

Rudolf of Habsburg followed the Babenbergs in making Vienna the capital of his realm. Royal protection, however, was not enough to spare the Viennese from all the horrors that were experienced by medieval cities in Europe. Fires, floods, earthquakes, and epidemics took their toll in the crowded and unsanitary streets of the old city, but the survivors learned valuable lessons in coping that have been passed from generation to generation. To this day, Viennese know the special art of "muddling through," known in German as *fortwursteln*. They will tell you, almost cheerfully, that things are catastrophic but not serious. The city's unofficial motto is *"Biegen, nicht brechen"* — "Bend, but do not break."

This popular wisdom was put to the test again and again. In the late fifteenth century, Vienna was occupied briefly by Matthias Corvinus of Hungary, and then in 1529 the Turks stormed the city with an army of almost 300,000 men. The enemies were driven back, but only for a little while. The Turks and their Hungarian allies again laid siege to Vienna in 1683. This time there was panic because the king, his court, and some sixty thousand citizens fled the city, leaving only a small garrison to protect the capital. All through the summer the siege continued. Just as starvation and disease were about to seal the city's doom, relief came in the form of armies led by John III Sobieski of Poland and the duke of Lorraine. Vienna was saved.

The Viennese like to say that they personally gained two lasting benefits from the Turkish siege. One was the introduction of coffee and of the coffeehouses that sprang up to serve the exotic

The elaborate marble *Pestsäule* (plague memorial) recalls the epidemic that raged in 1679, killing as many as 35,000 Viennese.

beverage. The other was an almond, butter, and sugar cookie shaped like the crescent symbol of the Turks and called *Kipferl* by the clever Viennese housewives who first baked them.

Having turned back the Turks and survived still another tragic outbreak of plague, the Viennese now saw their city grow in size and beauty. It was in this period that such eighteenth-century baroque architects as Fischer von Erlach and Johann Lukas von Hildebrandt designed and built the imperial winter palace, the Hofburg; the summer palace, Schönbrunn; and the splendid Belvedere Palace of Prince Eugene of Savoy. It was in these glorious years that the Viennese first heard the music of Haydn, Mozart, Beethoven, and Schubert — all of whom found some of their greatest inspiration in the imperial city.

The city was put to the test again when the French emperor Napoleon managed to occupy it in 1805 and again in 1809. But in 1814–1815, after Napoleon's downfall, Vienna was the site of the Congress that redrew the map of Europe. The impressive gathering of Europe's monarchs and their political advisers was remarkable for its festive spirit. The delegates danced to the tunes of composers such as Johann Hummel and Michael Pamer, attended concerts at which the works of such geniuses as Beethoven were played, and ate enormous amounts of splendidly prepared food. But that was only one part of the life of the delegates. The representatives who met at the Congress of Vienna are also credited with the fact that for nearly a century there were no great wars in Europe.

Of course, this was no guarantee that there would be no small wars or fast-spreading revolutions. In 1848 Vienna was touched by the first of the nationalist uprisings that signaled the beginning of the end for the Habsburg empire. In the same year, Francis Joseph (Franz Josef, in German) came to the throne. He forcefully ended the uprising by stern military action and by the promise of changes, which were never made. Yet, by the time the old emperor died in 1916, there was one thing that he had changed — the city of Vienna.

In place of the ring of walls, bastions, and moats that had protected the city for so long, Francis Joseph built a wide, tree-lined boulevard called the Ringstrasse, which does in fact circle the old Innere Stadt. Along the Ring, buildings of many sizes and styles but uniform imperial dignity arose, and Vienna was launched on its second great period as a home to creative geniuses from all over the empire and the German-speaking world. In the late nineteenth and early twentieth centuries, Vienna was the world capital of music because it was here that Johannes Brahms, Gustav Mahler, Richard Strauss, and Arnold Schoenberg composed some of their finest works. In literature it was the age of Hugo von Hofmannsthal, Arthur Schnitzler, and Robert Musil — to name only those men whose works are well known in English. In art this was the era of Gustav Klimt, Egon Schiele, and Oscar Kokoschka. Similarly, Vienna was a mecca for philosophers, scientists, and physicians who came to study at the university and in the laboratories and hospitals with some of the finest minds of the age, including the then almost unknown founder of psychoanalysis, Sigmund Freud.

And then suddenly the glory ended on the battlefields of World War I and three decades of trouble began. The once-stately imperial capital remained after the Habsburgs disappeared. The best minds of the succeeding generation fled to freedom from the

A proud imperial lion
guards the Hofburg in Vienna.

Nazis, who took over Austria in 1938. The misery grew through the war years — 1939 to 1945 — and did not truly end until the final treaty was signed in 1955.

Today the scars of Vienna's three most terrible decades are almost invisible. It is once more the serenely beautiful city that the Celts settled and the emperors embellished.

In the oldest part of the city there are traces of the Romans and of all their many successors. The ancient Cathedral of St. Stephen is not only a lesson in changing architectural styles but, according to curious custom, the burial place of the Habsburgs' internal organs. Their imperial hearts were preserved separately in the Augustinerkirche, and their imperial bodies were laid to rest in the Kapuzinergruft, the vault of the Capuchin monastery — both near the Hofburg.

Here in the old city is Vienna's oldest church, St. Ruprecht, and the still-older street named in honor of the Roman emperor and philosopher Marcus Aurelius, who spent the last six years of his life in the city. Nearby are the streets named for the bustling medieval markets — the Tuchlauben (Cloth Arcade) and the Kohl-markt (Cabbage Market).

Between these scenes from the remote past and the modern Ring is the Hofburg, once a palace and now a complex of museums, library, church, and splendid courtyards where the imperial guard once marched. The imperial dining room is still set as if the emperor and his retinue were about to enter to eat in its splendor, and in the Hofburg's *Schatzkammer* (treasure chamber) one can see the jewels, crowns, scepters, orbs, insignia, gowns, gifts, and ecclesiastical treasures that once belonged to the emperors. Still within the Hofburg complex, one finds the Augustinerkirche with its curious relics, the magnificent National Library, and the Albertina, which many consider the world's finest collection of engravings, prints, and drawings.

On the Ringstrasse side of the Hofburg are two beautiful gardens — the Volksgarten, or People's Garden, with its beautiful roses, and the Burggarten, or City Garden, with its famous statue of Emperor Francis Joseph as a stooped old soldier. Flanking the gardens on one side is the Burgtheater. On the other side is the State Opera, the home of the company that ranks with La Scala in Milan and the Metropolitan in New York City among the world's foremost opera companies.

The city's great buildings along the opposite side of the Ringstrasse include the university, the Parliament, the Rathaus (City Hall), the Volkstheater (People's Theater), and two great museums, the Kunsthistorisches and the Naturhistorisches. The art history museum, with some ten thousand paintings, is home to such treasures as Benvenuto Cellini's elaborate gold saltcellar and more than half the known works of the Flemish painter Pieter Brueghel the elder.

Specialists in nearly every aspect of history can find a suitable spot to satisfy their curiosity in Vienna. Among its many treasures are museums of clock history, fire-fighting equipment, folk art, and technology. Musicians must pause between concerts and operas to see the Viennese homes of Haydn, Mozart, Schubert, and Beethoven. And for those who like more martial things, the place to go is the *Heeresgeschichtlichesmuseum* — a very long word that may be translated as "army history museum." It houses a truly incredible collection of uniforms, weapons, banners, photographs, drawings and even the car in which the Archduke Francis Ferdinand was shot in Sarajevo (now in Yugoslavia) — the event that triggered World War I and the collapse of the monarchy to which the archduke was heir.

Having read so much history and seen so many palaces, churches, museums, and treasures, one almost forgets that a city is made up of people and that it is they who really give the place its unique character. As the citizens of the most densely populated and important city in Austria, the Viennese consider themselves special. From the time they learn to walk, the Viennese are surrounded by the stone mementos of their long past, and the city's history and its music are part of their daily life. Not too surprisingly, all this makes the Viennese more than a little sentimental. They think of their city more as if it were a beautiful woman than a collection of buildings and streets. The songs they dedicate to Vienna, *"Wien, Wien, nur du allein"* ("Vienna, Vienna, only you alone"), are love songs, and they do not feel the least ashamed if they feel tears welling up in their eyes when the violins play the melody. Having lived through so much, the Viennese thoroughly enjoy their oases of sentimentality and splendor — the opera, the Hofburg, the favorite coffeehouse, the *Heuriger,* or perhaps a few moments of quiet thoughts of what used to be as they sit in the shadow of Francis Joseph's statue.

The national tourist office describes Austria as "the most European country" — one of the few slogans that is correct. The tourist office likes to stress those things that Austria claims to have more of than any other European country — art treasures, castles, mountains, music, and so on. And although Austria does not have "more" people than many other European nations, the blend of nationalities and customs is a very important aspect of Austrian life. Austria's location in the heart of Europe made it a melting pot of different nationalities — a mixture that is still evident in all the provinces, but most especially in Vienna. A glance at the Viennese phone book or the names on store windows is like a tour of the old empire with its rich and sometimes revolutionary mixture of Czechs, Slovaks, Magyars, Moravians, Ruthenians, Serbs, Croats, Poles, and others.

To begin with what is almost a national pastime, eating, one discovers that time goes very quickly when there is the opportunity to eat six meals a day! The day begins simply enough with a first breakfast of coffee and a hard roll. It is assumed that hunger will return by ten or eleven o'clock in the morning, so *Gabelfrühstück* — fork breakfast — is served. At this meal one is expected to have meat or even the hearty Hungarian stew called *gulyás* —

The Most European Country

The Inn River flowing across a broad valley in Tyrol is just one of Austria's many attractions.

goulash. At the time of day when Americans grab a hamburger on the run, many Austrians still sit down to the main meal of the day. But this is not expected to keep anyone going for very long, even if you have worked your way through a menu ranging from soup to strudel — the airy pastry filled with apples or poppy seeds, cottage cheese, or cherries. Midafternoon hunger is relieved by *Jause* — that is, a cup of coffee and anything from a slice of buttered bread to a plateful of pastries, preferably with chocolate icing and a dab of whipped cream. Of course, many people have *Jause* at home or at their desk in an office, but the traditional place to enjoy this interlude is in a coffeehouse, where one can eat and gossip, or eat and read one of the newspapers the management thoughtfully hangs on racks for its customers.

The American dinnertime is suppertime in Austria. Supper is a relatively light meal designed to keep one in tiptop condition until after the theater or opera performance ends between ten and eleven in the evening. Weakened by all this pleasure, one must now have another meal, which can be anything from an open sandwich to an almost complete dinner, depending perhaps on whether one has just heard a Lehár operetta or Beethoven's *Eroica* Symphony.

Aside from the variety and quantity of food one can eat, the Austrian menu can be a tour through the old empire and history. One has a choice of hearty Slavic soups; Czechoslovak sausage, dumplings, and pastries; Hungarian dishes rich in paprika and sour cream — plus Italian spaghetti and ice cream. The historically minded may prefer a beef dish named for the Tyrolean countess Margarete Maultasch, or a soup named for a famous nineteenth-century admiral, Tegetthoff. Royal appetites are thoroughly satisfied with *Kaiserschmarrn* — a lighter-than-air pancake whose name means "emperor's fluff" — or simply the delicious little roll called a *Kaisersemmel.*

Austrian coffee drinkers also have an encyclopedic choice to cope with, in addition to what to eat at those tantalizing six meals a day. There are, just to begin with, *Mokka* (small cups of black coffee with sugar), *Kaffee mit Schlag* (coffee with whipped cream), or, for the courageous, *Doppelschlag* (with a double portion of whipped cream), not to mention the *Einspänner* ("one-horse coach"), a glass of coffee topped with whipped cream.

Along with the obviously imperial legacy of eating in great style, the Austrians of today have retained a number of customs that have their origins in the grandeur of the past. The use of majestic-sounding titles is one of them. For example, one may safely address any reasonably dignified-looking man as *Herr Professor* or *Herr Doktor,* and his wife as *Frau Professor* or *Frau Doktor.* The term *Exellenz* ("excellency") is heard a lot more than you might expect in a modern democracy. Specialists such as factory owners have their own title, *Herr Fabrikant,* but super-specialists — as Joseph Wechsberg has pointed out in his beautiful book *Vienna, My Vienna* — have titles to match their jobs. The virtually unpronounceable title for a Danube river steamboat captain is *Donaudampfschiffahrtsgesellschaftskapitän.*

On top of all this — like the whipped cream that decorates the coffee and pastries — Vienna offers an opportunity to learn a unique form of German. *Wienerisch,* the city's dialect, starts out as recognizable German but is as different from the German of Berlin as the American English of Mississippi is from that of Boston. It is a dialect full of music and humor. The ending *-erl* tacked onto

Austria's champion skiers begin practicing
when they are still very young.

nouns turns them into diminutives, so that *Buss* ("kiss"), for example, becomes *Busserl* in Viennese. Proper names are changed too, so that the dignified Carolina becomes Lini or Linerl, and you will rarely meet a Maria but many Mizzis. Even stately buildings are treated affectionately, so that St. Stephen's Cathedral is often called *Der Alte Steffl* — "Old Steve." Added to these characteristics are phrases that are used as often as an operetta chorus. Even a foreigner can get along nicely with the words *"Aber geh!"* to express a range of emotions from outright doubt to "Gee whiz!" If one remembers to drawl the German *"ja"* into "yaaw" for "yes," one is almost ready to enter the life of the city.

Clearly Vienna's German is a faithful reflection of the city for which it speaks. The Viennese are easily as hardworking as their German neighbors, but they have developed a life-style that is far less hectic, far less typically twentieth-century. The art of living, *Lebenskunst,* is as important in Austria as the traditional creative arts of architecture, literature, and music.

The appreciation of all the gentle arts is fully balanced by a busy calendar of traditional holidays and sporting events. Like most Europeans, the Austrians are passionate soccer fans and vocal supporters of their gold-medal-winning athletes. In fact, a recent poll showed that the Austrians ranked championship skier Toni Sailer as a national hero ahead of Wolfgang Amadeus Mozart — but, then, the Austrians are also well known for their sense of humor. It may be that the Austrians' sharp sense of the ridiculous has helped them to survive so long at their tormented crossroads in the heart of Europe.

Traveling through the provinces of Austria and enjoying their good life, one may easily become so fascinated by the mosaiclike details that one forgets that the tiny, colorful pieces fit together to form a complete picture. This picture is, of course, the history of Austria.

The restless centuries when Europe was settled were followed in Austria by nearly a thousand years under the rule of only two dynasties — the Babenbergs and the Habsburgs. Austria's history as a nation begins in 976, when Leopold of Babenberg was given the Ostmark as a reward for his help in putting down an uprising in Bavaria (now part of Germany). The Babenbergs' 270-year rule of Austria paralleled the growth of the tiny duchy into a prosperous nation. Under the Babenbergs the gold, silver, and salt mines flourished, producing wealth that was used to build the great monasteries at Melk, Klosterneuburg, and Heiligenkreuz, as well as to improve the nation's fortresses against the all too frequent attacks of its enemies. And it was in the reign of Heinrich II Jasomirgott (whose nickname means "So help me God," his favorite expression) that Vienna became firmly established as the nation's capital.

When the last of the Babenbergs died in 1246 in a battle

The Rise of the Empire

A museum at Carnuntum shelters the relics of the
ancient Romans, who made this town their frontier capital.

against the Magyars (Hungarians), Austria was again without a ruler. The king of Bohemia, Ottokar II Premysl, took this opportunity to expand his already large realm. By 1251 he had settled himself comfortably in Vienna and taken over the provinces of Carniola (now part of Yugoslavia) and Carinthia. This daring move by the Bohemian king enraged and frightened the German princes, who did not want the Slavs of Bohemia to get this close to their frontiers. Rudolf of Habsburg was selected "king of Germany" and told to drive Ottokar out of the German-speaking territory. Rudolf and Ottokar's armies twice met in the Marchfeld. In the decisive battle in 1278, Ottokar was killed. Rudolf was now master of Upper and Lower Austria, as well as the duchies of Styria and Carinthia, and the margravate of Carniola.

As the historian Richard Rickett has said: "The chronicle of the House of Habsburg in Austria is not unlike the course of a jet airliner: a relatively steep climb to maximum altitude, followed by a long and gradual decline." The steep climb began slowly in the fourteenth century with the peaceful acquisition of Vorarlberg and Tyrol, as well as Istria and parts of Friuli, in what are now Italy and Yugoslavia. The Habsburgs also extended their influence to include Salzburg, although its real rulers remained the archbishops.

The high point in Austria's expansion began in the fifteenth century during the reign of Frederick (or Friedrich) III, a strange man who has been called both wise and lazy. It seems that he was not a warrior but rather a clever strategist who concluded that the best way to build Austria was through the marriages of his children and grandchildren to the offspring of other European royal families. Frederick's motto *A E I O U (Austriae est imperare orbi universo* — it is for Austria to rule the world) was put into effect by the marriage of his son Maximilian I to Mary of Burgundy. Burgundy, now only a region of France that has given its name to a famous wine, at that time was a territory that stretched from Switzerland to the North Sea and included Franche-Comté, Flanders, Brabant, Zeeland, Friesland, and Luxembourg. Bloody wars were to be fought over these lands later, but at the time it seemed that Frederick III had hit upon a perfect plan, one that is commemorated in a famous Latin couplet:

> *Bella gerant alii, tu, felix Austria, nube*
> Let others wage war; you, happy Austria, wed.
> *Nam quae Mars aliis dat tibi regna Venus*
> The lands others win from Mars, you are given by Venus.

To cap his romantic and political achievements, Frederick was the first Habsburg to be crowned Holy Roman Emperor — a title that remained exclusively the Habsburgs' until it was abolished in 1806.

It was Frederick's son Maximilian who consolidated Habsburg power, of course, through marriage, by protecting it against the growing strength of France. He ensured the future of the dynasty by arranging the marriage of his son Philip to Juana of Castile and Aragon, in Spain, and of his grandchildren to the royal children of Bohemia and Hungary. Both Bohemia and Hungary were to remin part of the Habsburg empire until 1918, but it was Philip and Juana's son Charles V who was to bring the Habsburgs to the pinnacle of their power.

Charles, who was born in 1500, inherited the Austrian lands from his grandfather, along with the right of succession to the thrones of Bohemia and Hungary. From his father he inherited Burgundy, and from his mother, the vast Spanish Empire in the Old and New Worlds. Through the artfulness of his ancestors, Charles had acquired an empire upon which the sun literally did not set.

Charles had the wisdom to realize that he could not govern this enormous realm alone and gave his Austrian possessions to his brother Ferdinand to rule. From 1521 until the early eighteenth century there were two houses of Habsburg — a Spanish one and an Austrian one. Together they managed to stave off new threats from France and to drive back the first of the dangerous invasions by the Turks. The enemy that the devoutly Catholic Charles was most determined to defeat — the new Protestant faith — was not so easily turned back. The armies of Catholic Austria suffered severely in all their battles against the Protestants during the Thirty Years' War (1618–1648). Austria's sole important victory, against the Protestants of Bohemia at the Battle of White Mountain outside of Prague in 1620, tightened Austria's grip on the Czech lands of Bohemia and Moravia. At the moment it was a victory for Catholic Austria, but it sowed the seeds that would flower into full rebellion in the nineteenth century and destroy Habsburg power totally in the twentieth.

In the late seventeenth and eighteenth centuries the most obvious fact about Austria was not its instability but its enormous power. In the year 1740 Austria's most serious problem seemed to be one of succession to the throne. When the last Austrian male Habsburg, Charles VI, died in that year, he was to be succeeded by his daughter, Maria Theresa. It was not a plan that met with overwhelming approval in the unliberated courts of that day.

Fortunately for Austria, the new queen was a remarkable woman who somehow managed both to rule her vast empire for forty years and to raise a large family with her husband, Francis Stephen of Lorraine (in German, Franz Stefan). The skillful diplomacy of her chancellor, Wenzel Kaunitz, transformed the Habsburgs' traditional enemy, France, into an ally — at a time when Austria badly needed an ally to resist the rising power of Prussia under Frederick the Great and of Russia under Catherine the Great. Frederick the Great ruthlessly seized Silesia (a mineral-rich slice of land now shared by Poland and Czechoslovakia) from Austria in the early days of Maria Theresa's reign. Maria Theresa warred for its return, unsuccessfully, but apparently overcame her profound distrust of the Prussian military genius to share with him and Catherine of Russia in the equally ruthless partition of Poland.

The Decline of the Empire

The Habsburg Empire, 1815

Austria's share was Galicia, a relatively remote territory that was to be a source of grave trouble in times to come.

Maria Theresa's more positive achievements included the modernization and centralization of the large imperial government, financial reforms, and the drafting of a new code of laws. How best to rule the widely differing peoples in the vast realm was a problem neither the queen nor any of her successors managed to solve, although each of them tried to find the answer.

Maria Theresa's son, her co-regent after his father's death and emperor after her death, was Joseph II. Often called "the reforming emperor" and an enlightened despot, Joseph was in fact a rude, haughty, and impetuous man. But to his eternal credit, he abolished serfdom and torture in his empire, eliminated the punishment of heresy against the Catholic Church, and emancipated the Jews. Unfortunately, everything Joseph did — including such steps as imposing the German language and the Austrian bureaucracy on the Bohemians — was done so hastily and arrogantly that the result was a new kind of chaos. The nobles were upset, the Church was angered, and even the poor people Joseph tried to help did not gain very much. Finally even the well-intentioned emperor acknowledged that he had moved with more speed than wisdom. As his epitaph, he chose the tragic words "Here lies Joseph II, who failed in everything he undertook."

During his brief reign, Joseph's brother Leopold II provided the nation with a short interlude of serenity. Then, from 1792 to 1835, Austria was ruled by Francis I, a remarkable man who somehow managed to survive the onslaught of Napoleon's armies, the constant shifting of frontiers in his realm, and the loss of his title as Holy Roman Emperor.

Even Napoleon seems ultimately to have recognized that

Austria, while not an equal to France in battle, was still a European force with which to reckon seriously. And Napoleon did exactly what kings had done for centuries — he chose a Habsburg princess, Maria Luisa, to be his second wife. However, even this clever arrangement did nothing to change the tide of events, which now turned against Napoleon, resulting in his final defeat at Waterloo and the dismemberment of his empire. Under the leadership of Austria's astute chancellor Klemens Lothar Metternich, the representatives of some two hundred countries, royal families, and communities "cut up countries like old pairs of trousers," as the German chancellor Bismarck later said. Austria itself regained Tyrol and Vorarlberg, which Napoleon had seized, and became the chief power in northern Italy and in the so-called German Confederation. For the last time in its history, Austria was one of Europe's great powers.

On the surface, Austria — over which Chancellor Metternich ruled for the easygoing Francis I — was a peaceful and prosperous place. There were no wars, but there was also very little freedom for the people. In Metternich's Austria the Parliament, the newspapers, the universities, and above all the subject peoples — Czechs, Slovaks, Slovenes, Magyars, Croats, Poles — were suppressed ruthlessly at the slightest hint of a dangerously liberal or nationalistic thought. Before his death in 1835, the emperor Francis noted sadly, "My realm is like a worm-eaten house; if any part of it is moved there is no knowing how much of it will collapse."

Francis's son and successor, Ferdinand, amiably and, some say, simplemindedly, also left the care of the worm-eaten house to the aging Metternich. At last, in 1848, the years of repression resulted in a wave of nationalist uprisings that swept across the empire and into Vienna itself. Metternich fled into exile, and Ferdinand abdicated in favor of his eighteen-year-old nephew, Francis Joseph.

Francis Joseph began his sixty-eight years on the throne by thoroughly extinguishing the flames of revolution and promising changes that came too late to save the fast-crumbling house from total destruction. His triumphs — the rebuilding of Vienna and the tremendous artistic and scientific achievements of his reign — were overshadowed by a series of personal and political tragedies. His son and heir's suicide and his wife's assassination by a madman were the terrible personal blows he had to endure. On the international scene, the blows also fell, one after the other.

In 1859 Austria's army, under Francis Joseph's personal command, was soundly defeated by the combined forces of Sardinia and France at the battles of Magenta and Solferino in northern Italy. The result was that Austria's power in Italy disappeared almost completely, while Italy itself soon afterward became a unified and independent nation. In the north a new threat brewed under the banner of Prussia, which, following the traditions of Frederick the Great, was by now the leading military force in Europe and soon would lead the German states into unification. At Königgrätz in 1866 the Austrian army was soundly beaten by the Prussians — a clear sign of which nation was to be the major force among the German-speaking peoples.

Austria might have managed to survive all these blows and the terrible loss of prestige if some method had been found for uniting the peoples under Austrian rule, who, taken together, far outnumbered the ruling Austrian population. But, instead of giving all the subject peoples an equal status and voice in the gov-

A statue of the emperor Francis Joseph as an old soldier stands in a Viennese park not far from the Hofburg.

ernment, Francis Joseph, for a variety of reasons, singled out the Magyars for special treatment. From 1867 to 1918 the empire was known as the Dual Monarchy of Austria-Hungary. Francis Joseph now ruled as emperor of Austria and apostolic king of Hungary, but each of the two nations had its own Parliament, prime minister, official language, and subject peoples.

The Austro-Hungarian Dual Monarchy was a compromise that could not work. The Czechs with their long history of independence and their highly developed industry now redoubled their efforts to free themselves from Austria, as did the subject peoples everywhere in the empire.

Finally, on June 28, 1914, in the small Bosnian town of Sarajevo, a Serbian nationalist named Gavrilo Princip assassinated the archduke Francis Ferdinand, the heir to the imperial throne. For Emperor Francis Joseph, the archduke's murder was the final blow. To avenge the honor of the house of Habsburg, the aged emperor prepared again to lead his troops into war. But the war that began in 1914 and ended in 1918 was no isolated battle such as those of 1859 and 1866. It was a total war that engulfed almost all of the world. By the time it was over, Francis Joseph had been dead for two years and his successor, Charles (Karl) I, had renounced his rights to the throne his family had held for 640 years.

The small republic of Austria that emerged from the ruins of the First World War resembled a tremendously rich family that wakes up one morning to find itself penniless and dispossessed. For some people in this position, the effort of beginning all over again is too great and they give up. But the resilient Austrians, stripped of the widespread resources and markets of the old empire, with the economy gripped by inflation, somehow struggled to their feet in the early 1920s.

Unfortunately, events took place that finally overwhelmed the new republic. Many citizens who clung to the memories of the imperial past attempted to reinstate an absolutist government such as those that were growing in neighboring Italy under Benito Mussolini and in Germany under the leadership of the Austrian-born Adolf Hitler. The bitterness of the defeat in World War I was compounded and magnified by the Great Depression that swept across Western Europe and the United States in the 1930s. To the bitter cup of defeat was now added the final bitter dose — widespread unemployment. The promises of the Nazi leaders combined with those of Austria's own Fascist political organizations suddenly became almost irresistibly appealing. So only twenty years after its founding, the republic of Austria disappeared into the Nazi Third Reich. It took the wanton murder of entire peoples

The Austrian Republic

— including much of Austria's large Jewish population — and the wholesale devastation that accompanied World War II to turn people away from nazism.

The war ended officially in 1945, but Austria, which had been liberated partly by the Russians and partly by the Allied forces of the United States and Britain, was to be occupied by its liberators for another ten years while the victors tried to agree on a suitable peace treaty. Meanwhile, Austria once more had to rebuild its cities, its institutions, its economy, and its hopes.

Austria's postwar "miracle," as it is often called, has been based on the establishment of a stable democratic government. Austria is a parliamentary democracy, with the federal president acting as head of state and the federal chancellor as head of government. The president is elected for a six-year term. The chancellor is the leader of the political party with the majority of seats in the bicameral (two-house) Parliament. The *Nationalrat* (National Council), as the lower house is called, has the chief authority for making laws, while the upper house, the *Bundesrat* (Federal Council), has the power to review and delay — but not to veto — those laws. Each of the nine provinces has a governor elected by the provincial legislature, which is in charge of welfare and local administration, while most real government authority remains in Vienna.

The Austrian economy has grown steadily since World War II, providing its people with jobs that make it possible for them to maintain a relatively high standard of living. Close cooperation between labor and industrial leaders has kept strikes to a minimum.

Although the universities have still not fully recovered from the exodus of scholars in the 1930s, Austrian students receive a first-rate education — in state-supported schools, if they wish — from the first year of kindergarten to the last year of studies at one of the nation's seventeen universities or any one of the numerous academies where specialized subjects ranging from music to hotel management can be studied.

Against this background of stable government and prosperity, Austria is attempting to play a new role in international affairs as a completely neutral nation. Since the end of World War II, the Austrian government has chosen to guard its strategic location by acting as a bridge between East and West. Although this is infinitely better than empire-building or endless warfare, it is also an awkward role. Neutral Austria's most distinguished and successful voice is that of the secretary-general of the United Nations, Kurt Waldheim. Its least successful aspect has been the humanitarian but short-lived moments when Austria was a way station for oppressed peoples — Hungarians, Czechs, and Jews — fleeing from Communist East Europe and the Soviet Union. There are critics of Austria that feel the country should offer itself as a home rather than a way station (and sometimes not even that) to these people in flight from the eastern end of the bridge.

Clearly, modern, republican Austria has its share of problems, which arise, as they always have, from its location. But they are problems whose answers are suggested by a thousand years of history and shared traditions. Building for the future, the Austrians are reminded by the annual New Year's performance of *Die Fledermaus* at the Vienna State Opera of Johann Strauss's sensible musical advice: *"Glücklich ist, wer vergisst was doch nicht zu ändern ist"* — "Happy is [he] who forgets what cannot be changed." Sentimental sons and daughters of the empire may still place fresh flowers on the tomb of Francis Joseph, but most Austrians prefer to use the lessons of the past to build a better future at the crossroads of Europe.

Index

France, 53–55, 58, 59
Francis I, 57, 58
Francis Ferdinand, archduke, 42–43,
  61
Francis Joseph, emperor, 29, 39, 42,
  43, 59, 61, 64
Frederick II, king of Prussia
  (Frederick the Great), 55, 59
Frederick III, 52–53
Freud, Sigmund, 39

German Confederation, 58
Germans, 7, 10, 49, 59
Goldenes Dachl, Innsbruck, 11
Government, 63
Graz, 21, 23, 25, 29
Great Britain, 63
Great Depression, 62
Grossglockner, 17, 21
Gruber, Franz, 17

Habsburgs, 33, 34, 39, 41, 50, 52–
  55, 57–59, 61
Hallstatt, 29
Haydn, Franz Joseph, 26, 38, 42
Heinrich II (Jasomirgott), 50
History, 50, 52–55, 57–59, 61–64
Hitler, Adolf, 62
Hofburg, 38, 41–42, 43
Hofer, Andreas, 10–11
Holy Roman emperors, 4, 53
Hungary, 53, 54, 61
Hydroelectric power, 9

Industry, 9, 11, 13, 31, 32

Innsbruck, 11, 13
Italy, 52, 59, 62

Jews, 57, 63, 64
John III, king of Poland, 36
Joseph II, 57

Kaunitz, Wenzel, 55
Klagenfurt, 18, 19
Kranzelreiten, 21
Krimml waterfall, 17

Lehár, Franz, 29, 46
Leopold of Babenberg, 50
Linz, 29, 31, 32
Lippizaner horses, 25
Liszt, Franz, 26
Literature, 39
Lower Austria, 28, 31–34, 52

Magdalensberg, 18, 19
Magyars, 61
Mahler, Gustav, 39
Marcus Aurelius, 41
Maria Theresa, 11, 32, 55, 57
Mary of Burgundy, 53
Matthias Corvinus, king of Hungary,
  36
Maultasch, Margarete, countess, 10,
  46
Maximilian I, 11, 13, 32, 53
Melk, 33, 50
Metternich, Klemens Lothar, 58–59
Minerals and mining, 13, 14, 18, 21,
  23, 50